Little Green F:

Mary An Van Hage

Illustrated by Bettina Paterson

Photographed by Lucy Tizard

MACDONALD YOUNG BOOKS

For Jack, Theo and George

This book was prepared for Macdonald Young Books
by Wendy Knowles
Design, typesetting and layout by Chris McLeod

First published in 1995 by
Macdonald Young Books

Text © Mary An Van Hage 1995
Design and illustrations © Macdonald Young Books
Illustrations © Bettina Paterson 1995

Macdonald Young Books
61 Western Road
Hove
East Sussex
BN3 1JD

Printed and bound by Edições ASA, Portugal

A catalogue record for this book
is available from the British Library

ISBN 0 7500 1683 3
0 7500 2351 1 (pb)

For your safety

Have fun with the projects in *Little Green Fingers* –
but remember an adult should always be nearby
when you are gardening. Be careful when using
plastic bags and whenever you see this symbol

next to a picture or instruction, it means that adult
help is essential at that point – for example when
carrying the heavy dinosaur garden, punching holes
or handling fertiliser.

Contents

Suzy the Sensitive Plant

Sow seeds in February or March

This plant is so shy and bashful, that if you touch it with your fingertips, the leaves immediately curl up and the branches droop. The leaves also fold up at night-time, as if they were going to sleep. The Sensitive Plant's real name is 'Mimosa Pudica' and it is fun to grow this plant from seed.

Don't close the leaves too often or too roughly

At night-time it goes to bed

You will need

Mimosa Pudica seeds - from garden centres in early Spring

Seed tray - or foil tray or margarine tub with holes punched in bottom for drainage

Saucer or tray-for 'seed trays' to stand on

Seed compost

Watering can with rose or rinsed out pump action sprayer

For potting on when seedlings are established

Plant pots with saucers

Houseplant potting compost

Spoon

What to do

1 In February or March

Wash your container or seed tray. Fill it with seed compost to just below the rim. Gently firm down the compost. Sprinkle a few seeds over it, leaving a space between each seed.

2 Cover seeds gently with a thin layer of compost

Water gently, using a watering can rose. The compost should be just moist. Do not drown the seeds or wash away!

4

Seed growth or 'germination'

1 Place your seed tray in a warm spot

A warm windowsill or near a radiator at 20°C is ideal. If it is on a windowsill, take it off at night, or in cold weather and place it in a warmer spot inside the room. As well as warmth seeds need air and moisture to germinate.

They will not need light until they start to grow. Water when the compost starts to dry out. Do not water if it is still moist, or it will become soggy and drown your seeds! Never let the compost dry out completely.

2 Your seeds will germinate in 2-4 weeks

Move the tray to a windowsill as soon as the seedlings appear. They now need plenty of light to grow. Take them off the windowsill on cold nights. Continue watering carefully as soon as the compost starts to dry. Do not make it soggy. Plants grow towards the light. Turn your tray every 1 or 2 days so the seedlings grow upright.

When the seedlings are 5cm high transfer each tiny plant to its own pot

1 Fill the pot's base with houseplant potting compost

Gently ease each tiny plant out of the seed tray. Be careful not to damage roots or stems. Use a spoon to help.

2 Holding the plant gently, by its lower leaves, sit it on the compost

Do not hold or squeeze the stem. Fill the pot with more compost to just below the rim. Press down gently and water lightly to help settle the compost. Keep it in a warm light spot until new growth appears.

Looking after your Sensitive Plant

Keep it in a brightly lit spot, with some sun, at an ordinary room temperature. Let the compost dry out a little between waterings. Don't close the leaves too often. You may damage them.

Grow a giant plant, like Jack and the Beanstalk

Sow seeds in March

A giant sunflower grows very quickly into a huge plant from a single seed just like Jack's beanstalk! Start off by growing the seeds in little pots indoors, to give you tiny sunflower plants. Each one can then be planted in a sunny spot in the garden, to grow into a giant sunflower by July. If you have grown several tiny sunflower plants, you could keep some to sell at your school bazaar, or to give away to your friends.

The Sunflower's real name is 'Helianthus Annus' and it is a Hardy Annual. This means that it will last for a year and can live outside even during frosty weather.

You will need

2 or 3 sunflower seeds - the giant variety Helianthus Annus
Some little yogurt tubs with holes punched in the bottom
Seed compost
A pencil

For later on
A strong tall cane or stick
Some string

What to do

1 **Sow your seeds in March**

Fill your pots about ³/₄ full of seed compost. Make a hole about 2.5cm deep with a pencil and place 1 seed in the hole. Cover with compost and water well.

2 **Leave the pots on a cool, bright windowsill (at about 16°C)**

By early May your seeds will have grown into tiny plants. Check their soil each day and add more water if it feels dry. Do not make it soggy!

3 **Let the plants slowly get used to being outside**

Start by putting them outside on mild days, then mild nights. After a week, your sunflowers should be used to being outside and can be planted in a sunny spot.

4 **Water well in dry weather**

This means every day or every other day, even on dull days and especially when it is windy. If you give little pots of tiny sunflower plants to your friends, remember to tell them to plant them in a sunny spot and water well.

5 **Your plant will grow to 1-3 metres tall**

By July it will grow a huge yellow sunflower at the top of the stalk. Your sunflower is now so tall and heavy you may need to tie it to a strong tall cane or fence to help it stay upright.

6 **After your sunflower has finished flowering**

You will see the flower head has made masses of seeds. Leave these for the birds to eat or else you can cut off the flower head, store it in a cool dry place for a few weeks and harvest your own crop of seeds.

You cannot eat these seeds. The part you can eat is inside the strong outer husk. But if you store the seeds in a cool, dry place you can use them to feed the birds in winter, or save them for planting again next April.

Baby tomatoes

A 'dwarf' tomato variety, such as 'Tiny Tim' produces delicious mini tomatoes, has a small and bushy shape and is perfect for growing in a pot or tub. You can grow the seedlings in little pots on the windowsill, and then in early summer, when the weather is warmer, place them in a very sunny spot outside on a balcony, windowsill or in a sheltered corner of the garden. By July or August you will be eating your own home-grown tomatoes!

Plant in March or April

You will need

Dwarf variety of tomato seed-pick out the biggest seeds to use

'Seed compost' -let it warm up a little before using by keeping indoors

Little peat pots to sow seeds in

Seed tray to stand peat pots in

Drip tray or large plate to stand pots and seed tray on

Watering can with fine 'rose' spray

For later on

Potting compost

Liquid tomato feed

One 7-10cm flower pot for each tomato plant

One 17-20cm flower pot for each tomato plant

What to do

1 Sow your seeds in March or April indoors

Fill peat pots almost to the top with compost. Place a seed in each and cover with a very thin layer of compost. Pat this down gently and water lightly with tepid water using a fine spray.

2 Place the little pots in a seed tray

Put a 'drip tray' under the seed tray. Leave them in a warm spot to germinate eg an airing cupboard or warm room (about 18°C). Tiny seedlings should start to show after about a week.

3 As soon as the tiny seedlings start to show

Move the pots to your sunniest windowsill. Turn the tray every day to prevent the seedlings leaning towards the light and growing crooked. Take tray off cold sill at night and bring back into the warm room.

1 Feeding

Start feeding your plants when they produce tiny shoots, like little arms, called flower trusses. Feed them once a week with liquid tomato feed. Dilute it, then water it in. The trusses will become flowers first, then tomatoes.

2 Wait for warm weather then start to 'harden off' your plants

Begin in May or June by standing them outside in a very sunny, sheltered spot during the warm part of the day and bringing in at night. Leave them out for longer each day, provided the weather is warm until they are outside all the time. Water now whenever the soil begins to dry out. In July or August your tomatoes will be ready.

Your tomato plant does not need much space but it will always grow best in the sunniest spot you can find.

4 Watering your seedlings

From now on water with tepid water whenever the soil feels dry. When you see roots coming out of the bottom of the pots put a little compost between each pot to prevent the tiny root tips drying out.

5 Repot when 7-10cm tall

Fill base of 7-10cm plant pot with potting compost. Drop peat pot into it and fill in all around with compost, patting down gently. Water whenever the compost feels dry, keeping it moist but not soggy. Keep turning the pots every day.

6 Repot again when 15cm tall

Gently remove plant, complete with peat pot and any soil clinging to its roots, from its pot. Repot your plant into a 17-20cm plant pot as before.

Don't be a prize pumpkin! ...grow one instead !

Plant in April or May

Ready for Hallow'een

Did you know that pumpkins can grow to 90kg? Or that you could grow four or five pumpkins from just one seed? You will need a sunny sheltered spot in the garden to plant your seedling or else you can grow it in a tub, on a balcony or patio. But wherever you grow your pumpkin you need to allow about 180cm all round - they do take up a large space!

Pumpkins love warmth and sunshine, so the ideal growing spot is a sun trap, out of the wind

What to do

1 Growing your seedling

In April or May, fill a flower pot with seed compost. Push in 1 seed, upright, 2.5cm below the surface. Water and place on a warm windowsill. Keep the compost moist but not soggy. Wait for the shoot to grow to 10cm and to produce 2 or 3 leaves before taking it out of its pot and transplanting it.

2 In May or June take the seedling out of its pot

Place stones in the bottom of your tub, and fill with compost mixed with manure. Or fill the hole in the garden with compost and manure. Place the seedling on top. Mound the soil up around it, then water in well.

3 Place the tub in a warm, sunny sheltered spot

The seedling now needs lots of warmth and sunshine. It must be sheltered from the wind. Be patient and leave it to grow. Don't let it dry out.

You will need

Pumpkin seeds

Small plant pot and saucer or yoghurt pot with holes punched in the bottom

Compost for 'Seeds' or 'Seeds and Cuttings'

Watering can with fine spray

Some liquid manure or soluble plant food e.g. Phostrogen,

Miracle -Grow or anything similar

Either an old bucket or tub - or any container 25 cm in size or larger, with holes drilled for drainage

Stones or crocks for drainage in your container

Or a hole in the garden, 60cm wide x 45 cm deep

Farmyard manure if you can get it

Your pumpkins will be ready by September. You could eat them baked, or as Pumpkin Pie, or make a lantern for Hallow'een.

---

4 **Your plant will grow runners**

The runners will come to about 120-150 cm all round. Pumpkin fruits will form along these. Try and provide lots of space around your plant (ideally 180cm) and keep training the runners round and round in that space.

5 **Feeding and watering it**

Continue to water well. As soon as the fruits start forming feed once a week with liquid plant food, which you dilute and water in. You can also feed the plant through the leaves, by moistening them with the diluted mixture. Use the fine spray on your watering can.

When your pumpkin fruits start growing bigger, feed twice a week.

6 **Pamper your pumpkins!**

Never let the soil dry out. Always water with tepid water. Support the runners on bricks then they won't be damaged by hanging down. If it's windy make a little shelter.

11

Eggstraordinary Easter succulents!

Succulents are small plants with fat stems and leaves used for storing water, so they can live on much less water than other plants. Grow small succulents inside eggshells, and stand them inside a painted egg box on your sunniest windowsill. It is easy to take cuttings from succulents in the Spring and Summer and you can have fun growing lots of new plants in time for Easter!

Take cuttings several weeks before Easter

Display your Easter succulents with some little chicks, painted hardboiled eggs, and eggshells filled with posies of spring flowers

What to do

1 Several weeks before Easter prepare your succulent containers

Paint your egg box in bright colours. Slice the tops off your eggs and wash the shells out. Place compost into the eggshells, filling each shell almost to the top.

2 Take stem cuttings from succulents with an upright, tree-like shape eg. Sedum

Cut 2 or 3 pieces of stem from the plant, each piece about 5-7cm long, with lots of leaves. Remove the lower leaves leaving pieces of bare stem about 2 cm long. Push these into the compost in the eggshell so the cuttings stand upright. Water with sprayer to moisten compost.

3 Take whole leaf cuttings from succulents with large or pointed leaves eg. Crassula

Break off a leaf near to the base. Push the leaf end into the compost in the eggshell so that the cutting stands upright. Plant 2 or 3 cuttings in each eggshell. Water with a sprayer to moisten the compost.

4 Instant plants using ready-grown succulents

Take each ready-grown succulent out of its pot. Fill the base of the eggshell with compost. Place the plant inside the eggshell. Fill in gently with more compost. Water with a sprayer to moisten the compost.

Your cuttings will take several weeks to take root

Looking after your succulents

1 Place your egg box in a light, warm place

A sunny windowsill is ideal. Let the compost dry out between waterings then moisten again carefully, using a sprayer or tiny watering can. Do not overwater-remember there is nowhere for the water to go! In winter succulents like to be kept dry so water less often.

2 When the plants grow bigger

Repot them into small pots, in the spring. In summer, succulents like a warm, light place. In winter, they like a cool, light spot.

Mr and Mrs Grass and family

Plant any time in Spring or Summer

You can create your own family of crazy 'Grass People'. They're fun to make and decorate, and in a short time they will amaze you with their heads of bright green hair.

You will need

For one grown-up grass person

One and a half egg cups of grass seed

Pair of nylon tights (1 leg per grass person),or 1 nylon stocking

Scissors

1/2 litre jug full of sawdust-available from pet shops

Cotton thread-same colour as tights/stockings or a very small rubber band

Waterproof container to hold each grass person - eg. a plastic tub or a glass, about 6-7 cm in diameter

Felt and buttons or sequins and scraps of material or ribbon

Non-toxic waterproof craft glue

For a child-sized grass person

1 nylon pop-sox (child-size)

1/4 litre sawdust

1 egg cup full of grass seed

Everything else is as for a grown-up grass person

Your Grass Person's hair may need a 'trim' from time to time

What to do

1 Make tights or stocking 'tube'

Cut foot off stocking or leg of tight, leave a piece of leg 20-25cm long. Tie a knot at one end of this. Trim any material above knot. Turn stocking inside out so knot is on inside.

2 Pour grass seeds into the 'tube'

Make sure the seeds are in the middle of the tube. This will be the top of the 'head', from which the green grass 'hair' will grow. Pour in about a cupful of the sawdust. Press down firmly.

3 Now for the nose!

Take a clump of sawdust between fingers and thumb and push it outwards from inside the stocking. Take hold of it from the outside with your other hand, to form the 'nose' bobble. Tie up the nose with thread or rubber band. Trim any loose threads.

4 Pour the rest of the sawdust into the 'tube'

Press the sawdust down so it is tightly packed. Pull stocking tight around sawdust. Twist the stocking around once and tie in a tight knot. Trim the stocking above the knot.

5 Making the 'head'

Pat and squeeze the knotted sawdust tube into a round 'head' shape. Turn upside down so the grass seeds lie on the top of the 'head', ready to sprout as 'hair'.

6 Decorating the face

Cut out shapes for the eyes, ears and mouth. Use felt, buttons or sequins. Stick them on with glue. Add eyebrows, ears, or even some clothes!

With light, warmth and moisture your Grass Family's hair will grow

Place them on a light, sunny windowsill

Stand them in containers on a drip-tray. Water well. Pour water over the heads and fill the containers with water. Do not let the seeds and sawdust dry out. After the grass 'hair' has grown continue to water well. Keep the water level in the containers topped up. The sawdust will soak up water like a sponge, helping to keep 'hair' fresh and green.

15

Yum Yum gobble gobble, flies for tea!

How to look after Freddie the Fly Trap Plant

You will need

Small or medium-sized Venus Fly Trap-the best time to get one from a garden centre is late Spring or Summer

Cover for your plant in winter- large glass or polythene bag

Freddy is an insect-eating plant called the 'VENUS FLY TRAP'. The VENUS FLY TRAP uses its hairy, trap-like leaves to catch its own dinner! Its real name is Dionaea Muscipula and it originally comes from the swamp lands of Carolina in the United States. You can have fun growing one at home.

Late Spring or Summer

For repotting in Spring

Small pot

Special 'insectivorous' compost from a garden centre or some multi-purpose compost with a handful of sphagnum moss mixed in

What to do - in Summer

1 **Place your Fly Trap in a bright spot indoors**

Fly traps like average warmth. Keep Freddy out of reach of bright sun coming through the glass. This can scorch him.

2 **In warm weather**

Fly traps don't like to be too hot. Put Freddy in a sunny spot out in the fresh air. Then the sun's ray won't feel so hot and he can catch more food!

3 **Catch some rainwater**

Use this to water your plant. Keep your Fly Trap moist. Do not let it dry out. Do not overwater Freddy so that he gets soggy.

Brrr- It's Winter, Freddy is freezing!!

4 **Cover your Fly Trap with a large glass**

This keeps the air around it humid and warm. Take the cover off occasionally to let in air and get rid of condensation.

5 **Place on a bright windowsill**

Never let the compost get cold and soggy. Let the surface of the compost dry out between waterings. Keep at room temperature.

6 **Don't worry if the plant dies back**

It starts to grow again in the Spring. In Winter the Fly Trap plant is resting. In Spring take the plant out of its pot and plant up again using fresh compost.

Plants from pips - grow an orange inside an orange!

or a lemon inside a grapefruit

Citrus fruits like orange, lemon, tangerine, lime and grapefruit, all contain pips which you can plant in little pots of compost in Spring. When the seedlings appear, it is fun to plant them inside an empty orange or grapefruit, and let them grow for a while on a sunny windowsill.

You will need

Citrus fruit pips-soak them in water for 2 days before using

Small plant pot, and saucer to stand it on

Potting compost

Pencil

Plastic bag and twist-tie

2 or 3 citrus fruit cut in half

Knitting needle

Plant in Spring or early Summer

Your Citrus Tree could last for years, but won't make any fruit unless it grows about 1.8m tall!

What to do

1 In Spring plant your pips

Fill a plant pot with compost. Make a hole with a pencil about 2cm deep. Plant 2 or 3 pips then water lightly, so soil is just moist.

2 Place pot inside plastic bag

Tie the top and leave in a warm, dark place to germinate (21°C). This could take 3-4 weeks. If drops of water appear on the inside of the bag just shake or flick the bag, so the drops run down.

3 As soon as the shoots appear

Remove the plastic bag and place the pot in a light, warm spot. Water when the compost feels dry. Keep it just moist and not too wet.

4 When the seedlings are 5-6 cm

Take your citrus halves. Scoop out the fruit and make lots of holes in them, from the inside, with your knitting needle. Put a little compost in base.

5 Planting the seedlings

Remove seedlings from their pot. Place one in the centre of each fruit. Fill in all round with compost - try not to damage the roots. Firm down gently and give a little water to settle the compost. From now on water whenever the compost feels dry.

Growing a Citrus Tree

1 When the seedlings are 10cm tall or if any green 'mould' starts to form

Plant each into its own pot of compost. Your citrus will grow quickly and develop a good root system. In Spring or Summer, water it well and feed every 3-4 weeks with plant food.

2 You can put it outside in summer

Citrus love sunshine and fresh air. But remember to bring it indoors again before the cold weather. In Winter water much less and keep it in a light, cool spot. Next Spring if it is doing well you can put it in a bigger pot with fresh soil.

19

Christmas tulips

Bright and colourful tulips usually bloom outdoors in Spring, but if you plant the bulbs in late Summer or early Autumn, you can make them flower indoors in time for Christmas. Choose early-flowering deep red dwarf tulips, and when they bloom, decorate them to make a beautiful Christmas display.

Plant in August or early September

You will need

Bulb fibre - a special compost in which bulbs grow well

Red tulip bulbs - an early-flowering dwarf variety such as *Brilliant Star* or *Little Red Riding Hood*

Pots or containers - at least 10cm deep

Black polythene bag

Christmas decorations, holly, fir cones and ribbon

Blu-tack or glue for attaching decorations

Brilliant Star is a good red tulip to grow in little pots because it is not too tall

What to do

1 **Late August or early September**

Place some bulb fibre in your pots. Position the bulbs upright on the compost, so they are close, but not touching.

2 **Cover bulbs with compost**

Make sure the compost does not go right to the top of the pots or they will overflow when you water! Water well.

3 **Place pots in black polythene bag**

Leave in a cold, dark place - a shed or cellar for 10-12 weeks. Check compost now and then. If dry, add water. Do not make it soggy.

4 **When shoots are 5cm high**

Put the bulbs on a cool, bright windowsill for 7-10 days. Water carefully only if the compost feels dry. The shoots will soon be turning green.

5 **When shoots are 10cm high**

Move to a warm, light spot. Wait 2-3 weeks for your tulips to flower in time for Christmas. If you find your tulips are coming out too quickly move them to a cooler spot.

6 **Looking after your tulips**

Turn the pots every 2-3 days so each side gets an equal amount of light, otherwise the tulips will grow lop-sided. Keep pots away from draughts, fires or radiators.

Decorating your pots

Have fun making a colourful Christmas display. Choose from:

Fir cones or holly, left plain or painted gold, red, white or silver.
Christmassy ribbon - red, white, gold or silver.
Home-made decorations eg red fimo toadstools, felt Christmas
    trees decorated with beads and gold thread.
Group several different sized pots together. Try and keep to the
    same colours.

Hyacinth 'star' basket

Plant from early to mid September

Brighten up the dark days of winter with sweet-smelling silvery pink Hyacinth bulbs. Watch the roots growing in a glass jar filled with water or make your own Hyacinth 'Star' Basket.

You will need

Bulb fibre

Sphagnum moss

Prepared or 'forced' hyacinth bulbs. These can make your skin feel itchy, so wear gloves before touching them and wash your hands afterwards

Basket - at least 10cm deep, and a sheet of polythene to line it

Black polythene bag

Star-shaped stencils, coloured card, ribbon, beads, buttons and glitter

Scissors and non-toxic craft glue or blu-tack

Glass bulb jar or narrow vase

Silver and pink decorations look pretty with pale pink hyacinths

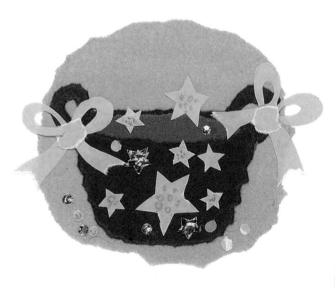

Have fun decorating your basket

Put moss round the bulbs to cover the soil. Tie on pretty ribbons and bows.
Cut out star shapes, paint them and glue on beads or buttons. Shake a little glitter over the stars to make them 'twinkle' and attach them to your basket with blu-tack.

What to do

1 **Early or mid September**

Line your basket with polythene and put some bulb fibre in it. Place your bulbs on the compost with the 'noses' up, so that they are close, but not touching.

2 **Almost cover with compost**

Leave just the 'noses' sticking out. Make sure the compost doesn't go right to the top of the basket or when you water it will overflow. Water enough to make the compost moist but not soggy.

3 **Keep your bulbs cold and dark**

Wrap the basket in a black bag and place it in a cold, dark, place eg a garage or shed for 10-12 weeks. Check the compost every week, and, if it is dry, water it.

4 **When the shoots are about 5cm high**

Take the basket out of the bag and put it in a cool, shady spot indoors.

5 **A week or so later, when the shoots are about 10cm high**

Move the basket to a warm, bright windowsill away from draughts or radiators. Keep watering, but don't let the compost get soggy!

6 **Turn your basket around every 2-3 days**

Otherwise your bulbs will grow lop-sided. If you find your hyacinths are coming out too quickly move them to a cooler spot. This will make the flowers last longer.

Hyacinth in water

1 Fill your bulb jar with water. Sit the bulb on the top, so it almost but not quite touches the water. Put it in a cold, dark place. Check the water level once a week and keep it topped up.

2 When the roots are about 10cm long and there is a yellow shoot on top, take your bulb jar out of the dark. Keep it in semi-darkness for 2 days. This helps to 'green' up the shoot and get it used to the light gradually.

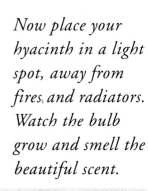

Now place your hyacinth in a light spot, away from fires and radiators. Watch the bulb grow and smell the beautiful scent.

Crocus on shells and pebbles

Plant September or early October

Colourful crocus usually flower outdoors in early Spring, but you can grow them on your windowsill much earlier, using just a saucer or a shallow container of water and some pebbles or shells.

You will need

Crocus bulbs

Small pebbles, gravel or sea shells

Shallow, leak-proof containers-such as saucers, sardine tins, old ash trays or large shells

Large flower pots or dishes

Strong, non-toxic craft glue or blu-tack

Pastel poster paints and brush

Scissors

Card, ribbon, shells and dried seaweed for decorating your containers

Blue, purple and white crocuses are easier to grow indoors than yellow ones

24

What to do

1 **In September or early October**

Wash the pebbles and shells. Place them in your containers. Pour in a little water so that it nearly reaches to the top of the pebbles and shells.

2 **Sit the bulbs on the shells**

Their 'noses' should be pointing up. Leave a small space between each bulb. Make sure the water level is just below the bulbs so they are not 'sitting' in water. The bulbs' roots will sense water is near, and reach out towards it.

3 **Leave the bulbs in a cold, dark cellar or shed**

Cover them with an upturned flower pot to make it extra dark and to keep away mice! The darkness and cold make the crocus think winter has arrived, so they make roots, ready for Spring. The water may need topping up, so it stays just below the bulbs.

4 **After 8-10 weeks when the shoots are about 5cm high**

Move your containers to a light windowsill, away from fire, radiators or cookers . Even if it is snowing outside the crocuses now think it is Spring, and will soon bloom.

5 **Making the flowers last longer**

Keep them in a cool spot. Top up the water if necessary.

6 **After flowering**

Don't throw away your bulbs. Plant them outside in a sunny, sheltered spot for more blooms next year.

The train now on platform 2

Plant any time

Make a Cress Train with each truck carrying its cargo of sprouting green cress seeds. They taste delicious in your sandwiches! Cress seeds can be sown any time of year and are ready to eat by the end of a week.

You will need

Cress seeds

3 or 4 small empty juice cartons

Cotton wool

Plant sprayer

Train and wheel shapes

Card and poster paints,

Non-toxic craft glue, scissors

What to do

1 Make your train trucks

Turn cartons on their sides. Cut off the tops to make 'trucks'. Paint the trucks in bright colours. Keep 1 carton for the 'engine'.

2 Make an engine and wheels

Draw round your train and wheel shapes. Cut them out and paint them. When dry, glue to the trucks.

3 Sow cress seeds

Wet some cotton wool. Place it in each truck so that the truck is half full. Sprinkle the seeds on top-thinly

When your train is empty, you can always sow some more seeds in the trucks

4 **Leave the seeds to germinate**

Place the trucks in a warm, dark spot. eg. an airing cupboard. After 2 or 3 days your seeds should start to sprout.

5 **As soon as the seeds sprout**

Put the trucks in a light place. Spray the cotton wool lightly to make sure it stays damp. Try not to spray the paint.

6 **When your cress is about 5cm high**

It will be ready to eat! Snip the seedlings with scissors and sprinkle on your sandwiches. Delicious!

When dinosaurs roamed the earth

Two hundred million years ago, dinosaurs lived on earth. Many of them ate only plants, despite their huge size, so they were herbivores. Scientists also believe they ate stones to help with their digestion! Now you can create your own prehistoric landscape, complete with dinosaurs, stones, and plants, in a fish tank!

Planting any time

Oblong glass container

Houseplant potting compost

Washed shingle, gravel, pebbles or broken crocks

A few handfuls of charcoal chippings

Small rocks, pebbles, pieces of bark or driftwood to decorate

2 or 3 larger rocks or stones for your 'boulders'

Plant mister spray

Model dinosaurs - the same size as some of your taller plants

6 or 7 small houseplants - those sold in 9cm pots or the tinier 'bottle' garden plants. Choose from:

'Tall, tree'-shaped plants eg Parlour Palm or any of the palms; Dragon Tree; Umbrella Tree.

'Bushy' plants eg Polka dot Plant; Boston Fern or any of the ferns; Desert Privet.

Small-leaved plants to cover the ground eg Mind your own business; Creeping Moss; Creeping Fig.

A Lithops or two would be fun - they are small succulent plants, called 'Living Stones'.

1 Making your prehistoric landscape

Place a layer of shingle, gravel or broken crock 18mm thick on the tank base. Cover with a thinner layer of charcoal and put compost on top, 5-7cm deep. Shape hills and valleys and position your 'boulders'.

2 Planting up

Water your plants well and make small holes in the compost for them. Ease them out of their pots and put them in the holes. Put taller plants at the back and let the trailing plants tumble over your 'boulders'. Fill in the gaps with the 'bushy' plants. Firm the compost round each plant.

3 Make your landscape look wild and rough

Put in more rocks, stones, and pieces of bark. Water it very lightly, enough to make the compost moist. Clean the tank walls with a damp cloth and polish them with a duster. Put in your model dinosaurs !

Looking after your dinosaur landscape

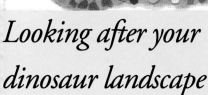

1 Put it in a warm room with lots of natural light ✋

Keep it out of direct sunlight. In summer hot rays of sunlight through glass can burn plants. Never put it near a south-facing window. Spray the leaves regularly with tepid water to make the air moist.

2 Watering your landscape

Only water when the compost is slightly dry. Let it dry in between waterings. Use just enough water to moisten the compost. Too much water in your tank will turn the soil soggy and rot and kill your plants.

3 Trimming ✋

Cut back long or straggly plants with a small pair of sharp scissors.

'Honey I shrunk the garden!'...

Start anytime

Try making your own indoor miniature garden with tiny, indoor bottle garden plants.

You will need

Place your garden in a light spot out of harsh summer sun. Keep the compost just moist. Only water when the soil is slightly dry.

Basket of gardening tools

Seed tray or any similar-shaped container

Washed shingle, gravel, pebbles or broken crocks-enough to spread a layer over the base of your container

2 or 3 handfuls of charcoal chippings

Houseplant potting compost

A little grass seed, moss, or turf for a 'lawn'

Pebbles or small stones, for a 'path'

Dried or artificial flowers

Fir cones, painted green, for 'bushes'

Mirror or shallow foil container for a 'pond'

Little house, people or animal figures

A few tiny indoor plants, sold as 'Tots'.

Choose from: 'Tree'-shapes eg. Palms or Ferns; 'Bush'-shapes eg. Creeping Moss or Peperomia or Croton; Low-growing, trailing plants with small leaves eg. Ivy or Creeping Fig; Colourful-leaved plants eg. Polka Dot Plant, Mother of Thousands or Tradescantia.

What to do

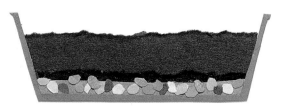

1 Cover tray base with a 2.5 cm layer of pebbles or shingle

Place a thin layer of charcoal over this. Cover with compost, 5-7cm deep.

2 Position any large items and make your pond

Place mirror on top of the compost or set a foil dish into the compost. Hide the edges.

3 Mark out a pathway with string

Fill in the path, using stones. Press the stones down firmly.

4 Choose a place for a 'lawn'

You can use moss or turf for an instant 'lawn'; or scatter grass seeds and water well. Your 'lawn' will grow in about 10 days.

5 Arranging your plants

Try 'tree'- shaped plants at the back and round the pond. Put trailing plants near the garden edges. Use 'bushy' plants to fill in the gaps.

6 Put in your plants

Make holes in the compost using a spoon. Remove the little plants from their pots and put in the holes. Firm soil round each plant. Water well.

Have fun decorating your garden with:

Dried or artificial 'flowers'
Neat rows of vegetables made out of modelling clay
Coloured fish, pebbles and water in your pond
Green-painted fir-cone 'bushes'
Vegetable frames - toothpick sticks tied together in a wigwam shape with little trailing plants planted at the base and tied to the sticks.
A model house, people, animals
Tiny plant pots

Useful information

List of botanical and common names

(They may be known by either one)

Common name	Latin name
Boston Fern	*Nephrolepis*
Creeping Fig	*Ficus Pumila*
Creeping Moss	*Selaginella*
Desert Privet	*Peperomia*
Dragon Tree	*Dracaena*
Ivy	*Hedera*
Joseph's Coat	*Croton*
Living Stones	*Lithops*
Mind Your Own Business	*Helxine*
Mother of Thousands	*Saxifraga Tricolor*
Parlour Palm	*Chamaedorea*
Polka Dot Palm	*Hypoestes*
Sensitive Plant	*Mimosa Pudica*
Sunflower	*Helianthus Annus*
Umbrella Tree	*Schefflera*
Venus Fly Trap	*Dionaea Muscipula*

Some succulent plants suitable for taking cuttings

Succulents from which to take stem cuttings:

Crassula
Flaming Katy (Kalanchoe)
Jelly Bean Plant (Sedum)

Succulents from which to take whole leaf cuttings.

Aloe
Crassula
Haworthia
Echeveria